Cougars

NorthWord Press
Minnetonka, Minnesota

DEDICATION
To all cats in the world, wild and domestic and big and little, with special affection for Scoop, Ginger, and Maggie.

Photography © 2001: Michael H. Francis: front and back covers, pp. 6, 8-9, 18-19, 30-31, 36-37; Tom Vezo: pp. 4, 20-21; Erwin & Peggy Bauer: pp. 5, 22, 26, 40-41; Wayne Lynch: pp. 11, 38; Tom & Pat Leeson: pp. 12, 32, 35, 42; Tom J. Ulrich: pp. 14-15; Brian Kenney: pp. 16, 24-25; W. Perry Conway: pp. 28-29, 34, 45.

Illustrations by John F. McGee
Designed by Russell S. Kuepper
Edited by Barbara K. Harold

NorthWord Press
5900 Green Oak Dr
Minnetonka, MN 55343
1-800-328-3895

Library of Congress Cataloging-in-Publication Data

Corrigan, Patricia, 1948-
    Cougars / author, Patricia Corrigan ; illustrations, John F. McGee.
      p. cm. -- (Our wild world series)
    ISBN 1-55971-788-2 (soft cover) ISBN 1-55971-807-2 (hard cover)
    1. Puma--Juvenile literature. [1. Puma.] I. McGee, John F. ill. II. Title. III. Series.

QL737.C23 C677 2001
599.75'24--dc21   2001022211

Printed in Singapore

10 9 8 7 6 5 4 3 2 1

Cougars

Patricia Corrigan
Illustrations by John F. McGee

NorthWord Press
Minnetonka, Minnesota

COUGARS are seldom seen and rarely heard. In fact, they often live their entire lives unobserved by humans!

But we do know that these members of the cat family live in eleven western U.S. states. They are found from the southernmost tip of Alaska down to where the California border meets Mexico and east all the way to the edge of Texas. Their cousins, Florida panthers, live in Florida. In Canada, cougars are found in British Columbia and parts of Alberta. Cougars also live throughout Mexico, Central America, and South America.

In different areas of the world, cougars have different names. They may be called mountain lions, wildcats, pumas, painters, fire cats, swamp lions, or catamounts. In Mexico, Spanish for cougar is *el león,* which means "the lion." And sometimes they are known by nicknames like "ghost of the wilderness" and "ghost walker."

Cougar eyesight may be five times better than human eyesight.

Males and females look alike, but it is the female that cares for the young.

Like all cats, cougars rest and sleep a lot, maybe as much as 15 to 18 hours each day.

Scientists who study animals are called zoologists (zoe-OL-uh-jists). They think that all cats and dogs may have come from a single tree-dwelling creature that lived 50 million years ago. Some early relatives of the cougar, such as the saber-toothed tiger, have become extinct, or have died out. They did not survive because their environment, or habitat, changed or disappeared.

Fortunately, cougars are able to live in many different habitats. Over time, they have adapted, or evolved, for living in places such as snow-capped mountains, jungles thick with vegetation, cool pine forests, grassy plains, and murky swamps. For instance, cougars that live in northern mountains tend to be larger and have a thicker coat of fur than cougars that live elsewhere. They learned to climb trees. And they also can swim if necessary, but usually prefer to stay dry—like their relative, the house cat!

Cougars
FUNFACT:

Native Americans have always treated the cougar with honor and respect. In times past, cougar skins were used to make arrow quivers and blankets. Claws were used to make necklaces, and sometimes tails were used to decorate clothing.

Cougars don't hunt from trees, but a high branch makes a good lookout spot.

The average cougar measures from 3.3 to 5.3 feet (1 to 1.6 meters) long and stands about 2 feet (0.6 meter) high at the shoulder. Adult male cougars weigh up to 225 pounds (101 kilograms), and adult females usually are slightly smaller. A cougar's tail may measure up to 32 inches (81 centimeters), almost two-thirds the length of the animal's body.

The cougar is one species (SPEE-sees), or kind, of wild cat. Cougars are medium-sized, along with bobcats and lynxes. Tigers, lions, and leopards all are larger and heavier.

Cougars are muscular and sleek, with little fat on their bodies. Fat usually serves as excellent insulation and keeps an animal's body warm. But because cougars have little of this kind of insulation, they have another natural defense against the cold: their fur coats keep them warm.

No matter the season, cougars are always alert to new things around them.

The layer of hair closest to the skin, called the underfur, is woolly and short. The top layer is made up of longer hairs, called guard hairs. These hairs are hollow and trap the air to keep cold temperatures from reaching the animal's skin.

Unlike humans, cougars have no sweat glands, so the cougars that live in warm climates cool themselves the same way dogs do, by panting to release heat from their bodies.

Cougars' coats are usually tawny, or orange-brown. They also may be gray, sandy brown, reddish-brown, and tan. All adult cougars have black markings on the sides of the muzzle, or snout, where the whiskers are. Some people say this area looks as if the cougar has a "mustache."

Cougars are just as active in winter as summer. The cold weather doesn't prevent them from moving very slowly and quietly.

If cougars were less secretive, scientists might be able to tell individual animals apart by the dark patterns on the muzzles, but few of the animals are ever seen.

The chin is white, as is the area right under the pinkish-brown nose. The tips of their tails also are black. The underside of most cougars is light, sometimes nearly white. At first glance, adult cougars resemble female lions.

Their coloring helps them blend in with their surroundings. It is good camouflage (KAM-uh-flaj) and helps them hide from their prey (PRAY), or the animals they hunt for food.

Cougars have good eyesight. In fact, vision is their best-developed sense. Researchers believe that they can see moving prey from long distances. The cougar's yellow eyes have large, round pupils that take in all available light. That helps the animal see at night almost as well as during the day.

A keen sense of hearing is important for cougars. They even can move their small, rounded ears to take in sounds coming from different directions. Cougars also have a strong sense of smell, which can really be useful when following prey. Still, their sense of smell is not as well developed as their senses of sight or hearing.

Cougars
FUNFACT:

A cougar is a "perfect walker." This means that when it's moving along slowly, each hind paw steps in the exact same spot where the front paw had been. When a cougar runs, it's not nearly as careful!

A hungry female with young to feed will even risk getting wet to catch a big fish for dinner.

The Florida panther is smaller than the cougars in the West and has longer legs, smaller feet, and a shorter, darker coat.

Like all of its cat relatives, cougars have whiskers. These sensitive hairs are also called vibrissae (vie-BRIS-ee). They grow on either side of the animal's nose and mouth, above the eyes, and sometimes on the chin.

These whiskers vary in length, but most of the whiskers found on the muzzle are long enough to stretch past the side of the face and back to the edge of the ear. The cougar uses whiskers to gather information through touch. With its whiskers, a cougar can determine the height of the grass, the width of the space under a rock, and whether a bush would be easy or difficult to push through.

Cougars make a variety of sounds, or vocalizations (vo-kul-ize-A-shuns). Their meow, which is a sign of contentment, is much louder than that of a pet cat. They also purr when they are contented. Cougars hiss first and then growl when they feel threatened. Unlike lions, cougars cannot roar. Sometimes the female cougar makes a whining or whistling call to alert males that she is ready to mate, and the male replies with a sound that is close to a screech.

Cougars
FUNFACT:

When watching or stalking prey, a cougar may make no sound at all. And it can remain motionless for long periods of time, even up to 30 minutes.

When a cougar sees an enemy nearby, it may try to look ferocious
and scare it away by showing its teeth and growling.

When running very fast, the cougar's whole body stretches out to cover a lot of ground.

The cougar's head is small compared to the rest of its body, but its jaws are powerful.

Like all cats, cougars groom themselves. Grooming helps keep their coats clean. They use their rough tongues to remove any loose hair and to untangle any matted hair. Female cougars groom their babies constantly, and young siblings have been seen grooming one another. Scientists are still unsure whether mating pairs groom one another.

Cougars have very strong jaws. And they have three kinds of teeth, 24 in all. The carnassial (kar-NASS-ee-ul) teeth are located on both the top and bottom jaws. They are long and sharp, used for slicing or shearing. The canine (KAY-nine) teeth are thick and sharp, used for puncturing. The incisors (in-SIZE-ors) are small and straight, used for cutting and some chewing. But cougars don't chew their food very well. They mostly gulp down large chunks.

Cougars
FUNFACT:

Sometimes cougars use their long tails to help them balance as they run. When they walk, the tip of the tail may drag on the ground and leave a trail, especially in snow.

Most adult cougars are solitary, which means they live alone. They protect their territory from intruders, including other cougars. Each cougar needs a lot of space, an average of as much as 200 square miles (518 square kilometers) for adult males and less than half that for adult females. They may walk as far as 30 miles (48 kilometers) in a day, searching for food or patrolling their territory.

While on patrol, cougars mark the boundaries of their territory by leaving their scent (SENT), or odor. Cougars may urinate on trees and bushes. Or they may scratch together a small mound of leaves and twigs, called a scrape, and then urinate on top of the mound. Sometimes cougars deposit piles of droppings, or scat, on top of the scrape. Cougar droppings may contain bone and fur. It depends on what the animal has eaten recently. The scrapes are left where they easily will be found by any cougars traveling through the area. Cougars also may reach high up a tree trunk and put claw marks into the bark.

Cougar habitat can be rugged and dangerous to travel.
The cougar's strong legs help it patrol for hours each day.

Large, older cougars usually make longer and deeper scratches than younger or smaller cougars.

Male cougars mark their territory for two reasons. First, they want to warn other males that this land is already taken, and newcomers are not welcome. Zoologists say that other cougars pay attention to these warnings and that rival cougars rarely come face to face. If they do, there may be a fight.

Second, males mark their territory to let females in the area know where to find them for mating. Because female cougars don't require as much space as males, they often choose an area that overlaps a male's territory. Female cougars are ready to mate by the age of two, and in most areas, cougars mate year-round.

After mating, the male and female each return to their separate territories. The female then searches carefully for a protected place, called a den site, where she will later give birth. Sometimes she finds a cave or an opening on a hillside covered by tree roots. Or she just uses a pile of brush in a hidden area.

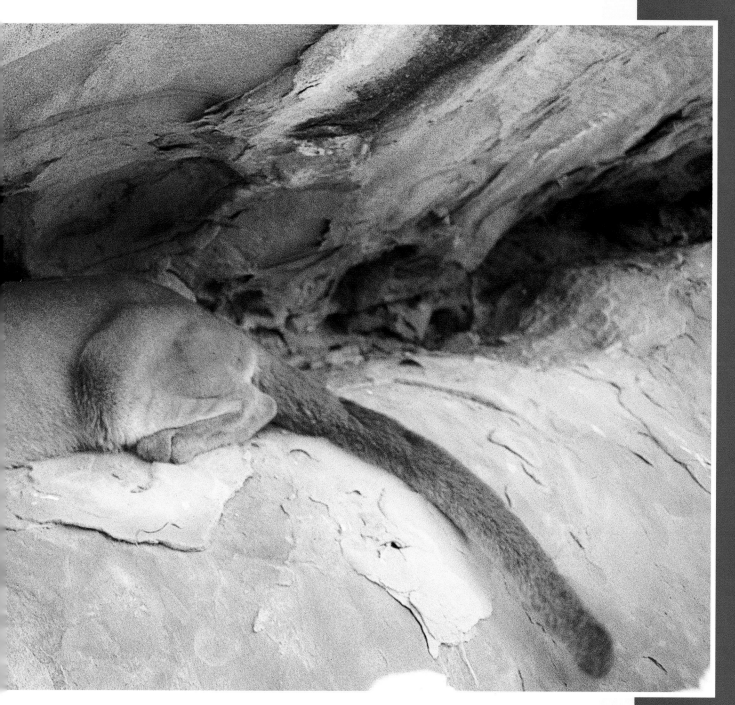

Small caves on rocky ledges make good den sites.
Sometimes there is only room for the young to crawl inside.

The baby cougars, or kittens, are born about ninety days after the female mates with the male. Usually, she gives birth to two or three kittens, but sometimes the group, or litter, is as large as six.

The newborn kittens have soft, fluffy-looking fur that is speckled with brown spots. This coloring helps camouflage them.

The spots disappear when the kittens are about eight months old. Kittens also have curly tails, which straighten out as they get older.

The kittens are born with blue eyes, which stay closed for about the first two weeks. Their eye color soon changes to yellow.

Kittens are totally dependent on their mother for food. They nurse for up to three months. Immediately after birth, and often in the next few weeks, the female licks the kittens to clean their fur. This helps them stay safe from enemies that might find the den site by detecting the scent of the newborn kittens.

Young kittens stay close to their mother for many reasons,
including food, protection, and warmth.

Mothers pick up their kittens by the scruff of the neck to move them one at a time to a new den site.

If a female cougar thinks that her kittens are in danger in a particular spot, she often finds a new hiding place and moves them. A mother cougar will do whatever is necessary to keep the kittens away from dangerous predators (PRED-uh-torz), or enemies, such as wolves.

When the mother leaves to hunt for food, the kittens stay hidden and quiet at the den site. When the kittens are about two months old, their teeth have grown and they nurse less. Their mother begins to bring them food every two or three days. The mother makes no special effort to catch small prey for her small offspring. At first, the young kittens just want to play with the food, no matter what she brings. One of the first lessons the mother teaches her kittens is how to eat this new food.

By example, she shows them how to bite, how to tear meat off the bone, and how to chew. She also teaches the kittens that their rough tongues are good for cleaning the meat off bones. After about six months the kittens are good at eating this food, and they begin to explore away from the den site.

The kittens stay with their mother for about eighteen months. During this time, she teaches them many things about surviving in their habitat. As the kittens mature, the mother cougar takes them hunting. They learn how to find and carefully follow prey. This is called stalking.

They also learn when to pounce, or jump out suddenly, to capture the prey. They are taught how to hide their kill and protect it from other animals. With a lot of practice, they learn to hunt for themselves.

Cougars
FUNFACT:

A cougar's hind legs are slightly longer than its front legs. Its paw print may be as large as 4 inches (10 centimeters) long and wide.

This young cougar still has some of its baby spots.
It is practicing stalking its prey.

Then, the young cougars go out on their own to find a territory and a mate. If they find good habitat with plenty of prey animals and water in the area, cougars may live about eight to ten years.

Cougars are carnivores (KAR-nuh-vorz), which means they eat only meat. They are expert hunters with strong legs for climbing and jumping and sharp claws for capturing prey.

On each foot, or paw, cougars have four toes. Each toe has a sharp claw about 1 inch (2.5 centimeters) long. Farther up the back of each front leg, cougars have another sharp claw called a dewclaw. This claw is curved and can be used like a hook to help bring down the prey animal. It also is used to help hold the carcass, or dead body, while the cougar eats.

Cougars may enter the water to catch prey, but they prefer to stay on dry land.

Most of the time the paw claws are tucked inside the toes. This kind of claw is called retractile (ree-TRAK-tul). Cougars walk on the soft pads on the bottom of their paws. They have four toe pads and one heel pad. Technically, they walk on their tiptoes, making little noise as they go.

When a cougar grabs onto prey the claws stick out. Cougars also extend their claws to get good traction when they run. They keep their claws sharp by scratching on trees.

Cougars
FUNFACT:

The Florida panther is endangered and rare. There may be as few as 30 adults living in the southern, swampy regions of Florida.

Cougars have good balance and can easily leap over fallen trees
and onto rocks without slowing down.

Tall grass that is nearly the same color as the cougar's coat
makes good camouflage for stalking prey.

Cougars can be active during the day and night. This means they may hunt for food at any time. They may hunt elk and moose, but their favorite prey is whitetail deer.

Like all cats, cougars stalk their prey. Once a deer has been sighted, for example, the cougar crouches down low in the grass or behind a big rock. The cougar silently watches, waiting for the right moment to pounce. The twitching of an ear or the tail is often the only sign that the cougar is there, and those signs are hard to see!

Once the deer is close, the cougar leaps from its hiding place and attacks. Like lions, cougars can run very fast for short distances, perhaps up to 40 miles per hour (64 kilometers per hour). Cougars also can leap 20 feet (6 meters) in a single bound, and jump as high up as 16 feet (5 meters).

A cougar usually attacks from the side or the rear, making the most of the element of surprise. It may jump on a deer's back, hanging on with its sharp claws. Then, with its powerful jaw, the cougar bites the deer in the back of the neck. That bite penetrates the spinal cord, and the deer falls immediately. When a cougar bites through the throat of the deer, the animal suffocates, or stops breathing, and dies.

Next, the cougar drags the carcass to a safe place for feeding. The teeth a cougar chews with are on the sides of its mouth, so it turns its head sideways when eating, just like a house cat. An adult cougar can eat 5 to 15 pounds (2 to 7 kilograms) of meat at one sitting. A whole deer provides meals for several days for a single cougar. A lone male may hunt just once about every fifteen days, but a mother feeding and raising kittens requires more frequent meals.

Cougars don't catch their prey every time. Sometimes the animal is faster and gets away.

Chasing a porcupine up a tree is one way to capture food.
But it's not an easy way to get a meal.

Sometimes the cougar hides a carcass from other animals by covering it with branches and grasses. Or it may dig a hole and bury the carcass as extra protection. Just to be sure no other animal steals its meal, the cougar may sleep nearby, in case it has to defend its food from bears or other large animals.

When deer are not available, cougars hunt small mammals such as squirrels, raccoons, chipmunks, coyotes, foxes, rabbits, marmots, rats, and mice. A very hungry cougar even will eat porcupines, which can be tricky because of the sharp quills. Those quills hurt when they stick in a cougar's soft nose, so the cougar has to be very careful! The Florida panther prefers deer, opossums, and wild pigs.

At one time, cougars lived in almost every state in America. Early settlers in the East did not like sharing the land with cougars, as the cougars killed deer that the people needed for food. To protect their families, settlers killed many cougars. As more people settled in cougar territory, the habitat was destroyed, and many more cougars died. Today, cougars are endangered, which means we must take extra care to protect them.

Conservationists (con-ser-VAY-shun-ists) are people who care about helping wildlife. Fortunately, they are working to increase the number of cougars and panthers. So, even though you may never see one of these secretive cats in their natural habitat, you will know they continue to share our wild world.

Cougars
FUNFACT:

Originally, the Latin name for the cougar was *Felis concolor* (FEE-lis CAWN-color), In 1993, scientists changed it to *Puma concolor* (POO-muh CAWN-color).

Cougars use their keen vision and concentration for watching over their home territory.

Internet Sites

You can find out more interesting information about cougars and lots of other wildlife by visiting these web sites.

www.atlantic.net/~oldfla/panther/panther.html	Florida Panther Society
www.discovery.com	Discovery Channel Online
www.kidsplanet.org	Defenders of Wildlife
www.mountainlion.org/Kids/kids.htm	Mountain Lion Foundation
www.nationalgeographic.com	National Geographic Society
www.nwf.org	National Wildlife Federation
www.panther.state.fl.us	Florida Panther Net
www.worldwildlife.org/fun/kids.cfm	World Wildlife Fund

Index

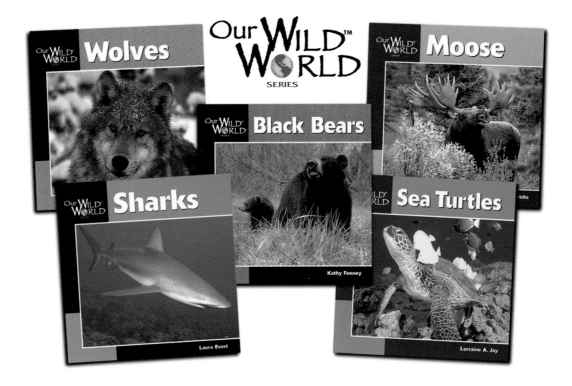

Paperback titles available in the Our Wild World Series:

BISON
ISBN 1-55971-775-0

BLACK BEARS
ISBN 1-55971-742-4

COUGARS
ISBN 1-55971-788-2

DOLPHINS
ISBN 1-55971-776-9

EAGLES
ISBN 1-55971-777-7

LIONS
ISBN 1-55971-787-4

MANATEES
ISBN 1-55971-778-5

MOOSE
ISBN 1-55971-744-0

SEA TURTLES
ISBN 1-55971-746-7

SHARKS
ISBN 1-55971-779-3

WHALES
ISBN 1-55971-780-7

WHITETAIL DEER
ISBN 1-55971-743-2

WOLVES
ISBN 1-55971-748-3

See your nearest bookseller, or order by phone 1-800-328-3895

NORTHWORD PRESS
Minnetonka, Minnesota